The Fight For Equality: The U.S. Civil Rights Movement

By Carole Marsh

Editor: Chad Beard ● **Cover Design:** Victoria DeJoy ● **Design & Layout:** Cecil Anderson and Lynette Rowe

Gallopade is proud to be a member of these educational organizations and associations:

The National School Supply and Equipment Association (NSSEA)
National Association for Gifted Children (NAGC)
American Booksellers Association (ABA)
Association of Partners for Public Lands (APPL)
Museum Store Association (MSA)
Publishers Marketing Association (PMA)
International Reading Association (IRA)

Published by
GALLOPADE™
INTERNATIONAL
800-536-2GET
www.gallopade.com

CAROLE MARSH BOOKS

1

Other Carole Marsh Books

Orville & Wilbur Wright . . . Step Out Into The Sky!
Lewis & Clark Go On a Hike: The Story of the Corps of Discovery
"What A Deal!": The Louisiana Purchase
How Our Nation Was Born: The American Revolution
When Brother Fought Brother: The American Civil War
The Fight For Equality: The U.S. Civil Rights Movement

State Stuff™, Available for all 50 states:

My First Pocket Guide	The State Coloring Book
State My First Book	The Big Reproducible Activity Book
State Wheel of Fortune Gamebook	State Millionaire Gamebook
State Survivor Gamebook	State Project Books
State Illustrated Timelines	Jeopardy: Answers & Questions About
"Jography!": A Fun Run Through Our State	Our State

1,000 Readers™

Orville and Wilbur Wright	Meriwether Lewis & William Clark	Sacagawea
Louisiana Purchase	George Washington	Paul Revere
Benjamin Franklin	Ulysses S. Grant	Robert E. Lee
Martin Luther King, Jr	Rosa Parks	Thurgood Marshall

Patriotic Favorites™

Patriotic Favorites Coloring Book	Young Patriots Coloring & Activity Book
Patriotic Biographies	Patriotic Projects
The Daily Patriot: 365 Quotations	Patriotism: 365 Definitions

Table of Contents

A Word From the Author ....page 4

A Timeline of Events ....page 5

The Fight For Equality: The U.S. Civil Rights Movement ....page 6

Revolutionary Rights! ....page 8

The Underground Railroad ....page 9

Slavery Has Got to Go! ....page 10

A "Little Woman" with a Big Book ....page 11

Lincoln Against Slavery ....page 12

Emancipation Proclamation ....page 13

Equal Protection under the Law ....page 14

Buffalo Soldiers ....page 15

"Jim Crow" Laws ....page 16

Women Fight for Equal Rights ....page 17

Indian Citizenship Act ....page 18

Tuskegee Airmen ....page 19

Japanese Internment Camps / Jackie Robinson ....page 20

Little Rock Nine ....page 21

Mother of the Civil Rights Movement ....page 22

Sit-in Protests ....page 23

Freedom Rides ....page 24

March on Washington ....page 25

Civil Rights Leaders ....page 26

Civil Rights Act ....page 27

Affirmative Action ....page 28

When Will It End? ....page 29

Additional Resources ....page 30

Glossary ....page 31

Answer Key/Index ....page 32

A Word From the Author

Dear Reader,

The Civil Rights Movement is a controversial time period in our nation's history. Sometimes it can be difficult to talk about it. But, like any time period in history, those who don't learn from it are doomed to repeat it!

Yes, the Civil Rights Movement can be difficult to study. Many people suffered for what they believed so that later generations could benefit from their sacrifice. But let's not forget the good that has come from the Civil Rights Movement. Many things in the United States have changed! The Civil Rights Movement brought an end to segregation, unfair voting practices, and other unfair treatments of minorities in the United States. Or has it? Today, we are living with many of the benefits of the Civil Rights Movement, but some say we have a long way to go.

Here is a warning for you: Do NOT forget the Civil Rights Movement. The Civil Rights Movement is a reminder that Americans must protect the basic rights of every individual now and forever!

Carole Marsh

4

A Timeline of Events

1776 – Thomas Jefferson writes: "...All men are created equal...."

1808 – Importation of slaves banned; illegal slave trade continues.

1852 – Uncle Tom's Cabin is published by Harriet Beecher Stowe.

1863 – President Lincoln issues Emancipation Proclamation freeing "all slaves in areas still in rebellion."

1875 – Congress passes civil rights act granting equal rights in public accommodations and jury duty.

1909 – Founding of the National Association for the Advancement of Colored People (NAACP).

1920 – Nineteenth Amendment gives women the right to vote.

1924 – Citizenship Act makes every American Indian a U.S. citizen.

1948 – President Truman issues executive order outlawing segregation in U.S. military.

1954 – U.S. Supreme Court declares school segregation unconstitutional.

1955 – Rosa Parks refuses to move to the back of a Montgomery, Alabama, bus; boycott follows and bus segregation ordinance is declared unconstitutional.

1957 – Arkansas governor uses National Guard to block nine black students from attending Central High School in Little Rock.

1961 – Freedom Rides begin from Washington, D.C., into Southern states.

1963 – Dr. Martin Luther King Jr. delivers "I Have a Dream" speech to hundreds of thousands at the March on Washington.

1964 – Congress passes Civil Rights Act declaring discrimination based on race illegal.

1968 – Martin Luther King Jr. assassinated in Memphis, Tennessee.

1983 – Martin Luther King Jr. federal holiday established.

1996 – Supreme Court rules consideration of race in creating congressional districts is unconstitutional.

2003 – Supreme Court reaffirms Affirmative Action in a case regarding college admission.

The Fight For Equality: The U.S. Civil Rights Movement

For many years, not all people in America were treated equally. In a democracy, "the majority rules." In America, that was also true. The Civil Rights Movement changed America during the twentieth century. While "the majority rules," Americans cannot ignore the rights of the minority. The Civil Rights Movement changed segregation, unfair voting practices, and other unfair treatments of minority groups in America. The Civil Rights Movement is a reminder that Americans must protect the basic rights of every individual now and forever.

Revolutionary Rights!

Before the United States became a country, people in the thirteen colonies began fighting for their "civil rights." However, even though Thomas Jefferson wrote, "...all men are created equal...," it would be many years before minorities and women would see the same equal treatment as white men. But that didn't stop minorities and women from becoming important leaders during the American Revolution!

Crispus Attucks

Crispus Attucks was born into slavery but ran away as a young man. He was living in Boston at the time of the Boston Massacre. He and four other patriots were shot and killed while protesting British laws. Paul Revere made a famous picture he titled, "The Boston Massacre." In it he showed Attucks lying dead. The death of Attucks inspired others to start the American Revolution.

Phillis Wheatley

Phillis Wheatley is considered to be the first important black writer in the United States. She was only a girl when she was brought from Africa in 1761. She

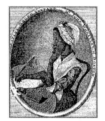

became a house slave for the Boston merchant John Wheatley and his wife Susanna. They thought Phillis was very smart, so they taught her and encouraged her to write. Her first book of poetry was published in 1773. She impressed many people with her patriotic writing. (After reading her work, even George Washington wanted to meet her!)

Fact or Opinion

Label each of these statements. Write F next to each statement that is a fact. Write O next to each statement that is an opinion.

_____ 1. Crispus Attucks was born into slavery.

_____ 2. Patriots should not have caused trouble for the British.

_____ 3. Crispus Attucks was killed at the Boston Massacre.

_____ 4. Phillis Wheatley was a writer.

_____ 5. Phillis Wheatley was the greatest black writer in history.

_____ 6. People were inspired by the writing of Phillis Wheatley.

FAST FACT!

The framers of the Constitution thought it would be wise to include the Bill of Rights to make sure that individual rights would be protected.

The Underground Railroad

Harriet Tubman helped hundreds of slaves to escape toward the North for freedom. The fugitives traveled on the "Underground Railroad." The "railroad" was a network of homes owned by people who were friendly to runaway slaves. Harriet also helped the Union Army during the Civil War. She was a spy!

The "friendly" houses below are marked with letters. Starting in the South, follow the trail to find the secret word. Color the friendly houses.

The "friendly" houses below are marked with letters. Starting in the South, follow the trail to find the secret word. Color the friendly houses.

The secret word is:

_____ _____ _____ _____ _____ _____ _____

Slavery Has Got to Go!

People who tried to get rid of slavery were called abolitionists. They began their fight against slavery years before the Civil Rights Movement began. Abolitionists wanted to see slaves go free. They campaigned to end slavery. They brought national attention to the abolitionist movement. Many of them broke the law at the time for what they believed was right. Some lost their lives so that others might have a chance for freedom.

Match the abolitionist leader with his or her description.

1. Nat Turner

2. John Brown

3. Harriet Tubman

4. Frederick Douglass

5. Harriet Beecher Stowe

6. William Lloyd Garrison

7. Sojourner Truth

8. John Greenleaf Whittier

A. Famous abolitionist poet from New England

B. Led a raid on the U.S. Armory at Harper's Ferry, Virginia (Present-day West Virginia)

C. Became the most famous leader of the Underground Railroad

D. Led a revolt against plantation owners in Virginia

E. Former slave who became a famous public speaker

F. Author of antislavery novel, *Uncle Tom's Cabin*

G. Isabella Baumfree changed her name to match her goals

H. Published abolitionist newspaper, *The Liberator*

WORD DEFINITION

slavery: involuntary subjection to another or others

10

A "Little Woman" with a Big Book

Harriet Beecher Stowe moved from Connecticut to Cincinnati, Ohio in 1833. There she became an abolitionist. Her novel *Uncle Tom's Cabin*, published in 1852, made a powerful statement against slavery. The book, a popular stage version of the story, and "Tom Shows" based on the story inspired antislavery feelings in the North. Many of the characters and events in the novel were based on experiences the author had while in Ohio or on stories shared with her by her family.

Uncle Tom's Cabin is sometimes considered one of the causes of the Civil War. During the war, it was reported that when Abraham Lincoln was introduced to Harriet Beecher Stowe, he called her "the 'little woman' who wrote the book that started this great war." One of the reasons for fighting the Civil War was slavery. The book raised public awareness of slavery and began to move people to join the cause against slavery.

Josiah Henson spent thirty years on a plantation in Maryland before he escaped slavery. He became a preacher, abolitionist, and lecturer. He also helped ex-slaves become successful farmers in Canada. His autobiography was published in 1849. After reading his book, Harriet Beecher Stowe was inspired to write *Uncle Tom's Cabin* using Henson as the model for her character Uncle Tom.

Pretend that you are a famous author. What would you write to change someone's ideas about something that is unfair today?

_____

_____

_____

_____

_____

_____

_____

Lincoln Against Slavery

In 1860, Abraham Lincoln was elected president of the United States. Lincoln was against slavery. By the time he actually became president, seven southern states had seceded from the Union. They wanted to preserve the institution of slavery.

These states formed a separate government. They called this government the Confederate States of America. Lincoln insisted that secession was illegal. He swore that he would protect federal possessions located in the South.

In December 1860, South Carolina seceded from the Union. Within a few weeks, Mississippi, Florida, Alabama, Georgia, Louisiana, and Texas also seceded. In April 1861, Virginia seceded from the Union. Later that year, Arkansas, Tennessee, and North Carolina also seceded forming an eleven-state Confederacy.

All of the states that seceded from the Union were slave states.

Label each of the states that seceded from the Union.

THE UNITED STATES, 1861

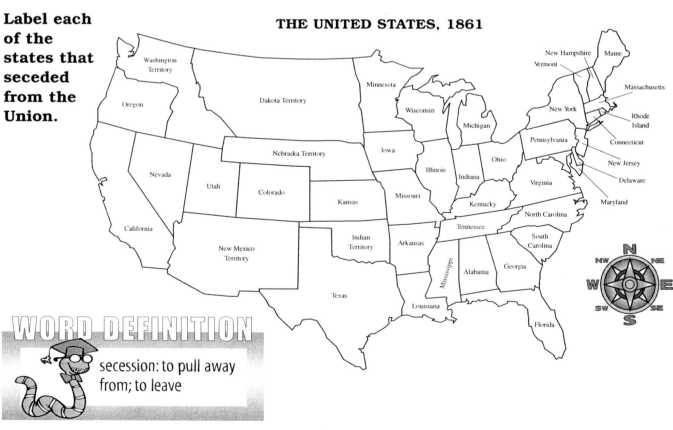

WORD DEFINITION

secession: to pull away from; to leave

Emancipation Proclamation

President Abraham Lincoln delivered the Emancipation Proclamation on January 1, 1863 during the Civil War. He declared that all slaves under Confederate control were free! Slavery was one of the main reasons why the Northern and Southern states fought each other. After being set free, around 200,000 black men joined the Union army to fight. Almost 40,000 black soldiers died serving their country in the Civil War.

WORD BANK			
1863	EMANCIPATION	SOLDIERS	CIVIL
FREED	SLAVES	ILLEGAL	UNION
SOUTHERN	ABRAHAM	40,000	

Use the "Word Bank" to answer the questions below.

1. The _____ Proclamation _____ the black _____ in America!

2. Once President _____ Lincoln delivered his famous proclamation, owning slaves was _____.

3. After gaining their freedom, black men could fight as _____ in the _____ army.

4. Nearly _____ black soldiers died in the Civil War.

5. The _____ War was fought between the Northern and _____ states.

6. The Emancipation Proclamation was delivered in January of _____.

Juneteenth is a celebration to remember the Emancipation Proclamation. African Americans celebrate Juneteenth in much the same style as the Fourth of July.

Equal Protection under the Law

   Before the Civil War, many courts were divided on how to treat slaves. Slaves were often treated like property without any rights at all. But other times, they were given a trial or made to appear in court as witnesses.

   After the Civil War, the laws were changed to reflect a new way of life for slaves. Many former slaves became landowners, began to vote, and even ran for office.

   The 13th, 14th, and 15th Amendments to the Constitution of the United States of America address the issues of slavery and guarantee equal protection under the law for all citizens.

● **13TH AMENDMENT:** Bans slavery in the United States and any of its territories

● **14TH AMENDMENT:** Grants citizenship to all persons born in the United States and guarantees them equal protection under the law

● **15TH AMENDMENT:** Ensures all citizens the right to vote regardless of race or color or previous condition of servitude (former slaves)

Answer the following questions.

1. Which amendment banned slavery in the United States?

   _____

2. Which amendment ensures all citizens the right to vote regardless of race?

   _____

3. Which amendment grants citizenship to all persons born in the United States?

   _____

4. How did life for slaves change after the Civil War?

   _____

14

Buffalo Soldiers

In the 1800s, many African Americans went west as farmers, settlers, cowboys, and gunfighters. They also fought in the Civil War. On July 17, 1863, African American soldiers helped the Union win the Battle of Honey Springs (Battle of Elk Creek).

Blacks suffered discrimination in the Army. Black soldiers received $7 monthly pay, but white soldiers were paid $13 a month. Blacks strongly protested against the unfair pay rate. Congress changed the law in 1864 to require that black and white soldiers earn equal pay.

After the Civil War ended, Congress passed a bill that created two African American infantry units. They fought cattle thieves, bandits, and Mexican revolutionaries. They also fought in the Indian wars toward the end of the 1800s. These brave men were called "Buffalo Soldiers" by the Indians because of their tightly curled hair, which reminded the Indians of a buffalo's coat.

Answer the following questions.

1. Why did many African Americans go west? _____

2. What battle did they help the Union win?

   _____

3. What did black soldiers protest during the Civil War? _____

4. What were these soldiers called by the Indians?

   _____

5. Who did the black soldiers fight against? _____

Find out more about the
Buffalo Soldiers at:
http://www.buffalosoldiers.com/

15

"Jim Crow" Laws

Scenes such as this one were quite common—especially in the South.

Jim Crow laws were a form of legal segregation. The laws made it legal to discriminate against African Americans in many communities and states. These laws made it legal to provide unequal opportunities in housing, work, education, and government mostly for African Americans, but for other minorities as well.

There were many African American leaders who spoke out against Jim Crow laws. They agreed that something should be done about them. However, they disagreed on what exactly should be done.

Booker T. Washington (1856–1915)
Washington stated he believed it was foolish for blacks to fight for civil rights before they had attained economic equality. He pleased many whites and gained financial support for his school, but many African American leaders disagreed with him.

W.E.B Du Bois (1868–1963)
Du Bois was a co-founder of the Niagara Movement, which became the National Association for the Advancement of Colored People (NAACP) in 1909. Du Bois demanded that African Americans achieve economic equality as well as full and immediate civil and political equality.

Marcus Garvey (1887–1940)
Marcus Garvey wanted to inspire all people of African ancestry to "redeem" Africa, and for the European colonial powers to leave Africa. Garvey was born in Jamaica, but lived in New York City for a time.

Answer the following questions.

1. What were Jim Crow laws? _____

2. What did Booker T. Washington believe that blacks should achieve before fighting for civil rights? _____

3. Which association did W.E.B. Du Bois help co-found? _____

4. Marcus Garvey wanted who to leave Africa? _____

Women Fight for Equal Rights

Before the 19th Amendment to the United States Constitution, women were unable to vote in all parts of the United States. In 1920, enough states ratified the 19th Amendment and it became the law of the land. Women gained suffrage nationally. Women today continue to be a major force in the election process.

Suffragettes parading down the street in 1917.

Match each word with its definitions.

1. Amendment   A. The right to vote

2. Ratify   B. People who could not vote in the United States until 1920

3. Constitution   C. An addition to the U.S. Constitution

4. Election   D. The selection, by vote, of a candidate for office

5. Suffrage   E. To give approval

6. Women   F. The fundamental law of the United States that was framed in 1787 and put into effect in 1789

Write a message on the sign provided that will help the protesters in the picture gain equal rights.

WORD DEFINITION

Suffrage: the right to vote

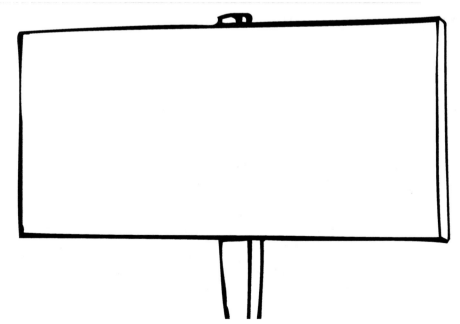

17

Indian Citizenship Act

On June 2, 1924, Congress granted citizenship to all Native Americans born in the United States. Because the right to vote was governed by state law, until 1948 some states barred Native Americans from voting.

> *"All non citizen Indians born within the territorial limits of the United States be, and they are hereby, declared to be citizens of the United States!"*

Number the following events in the correct order.

_____ 15th Amendment ensures all citizens the right to vote regardless of race or color. (1870)

_____ The U.S. Constitution describes the political process including voting. (1789)

_____ 19th Amendment states citizens will not be denied the right to vote on account of sex. (1920)

_____ Indian Citizenship Act makes Indians citizens and gives Indians the right to vote. (1924)

_____ Congress passes Civil Rights Act declaring discrimination based on race illegal. (1964)

President Calvin Coolidge with four Osage Indians

Osage Indians at White House

Tuskegee Airmen

During World War II, many black men left homes and on farms and in towns and cities across America to volunteer as Tuskegee Airmen. They were the first black military airmen to serve in the United States armed forces. After graduating from air training, many Tuskegee Airmen became pilots, navigators, or bombardiers. Some airmen became officers, and many served in supporting ground positions.

The Tuskegee Airmen faced doubt, war, and racial discrimination. Many white Americans thought black men did not have much intelligence, courage, or patriotism. But the black airmen proved them wrong!

Follow the directions to build a paper airplane! Use the pictures to help guide your steps. Fold an 8 1/2 x 11" sheet of paper in half lengthwise. Next, fold down the corners as shown. Then fold each side down to the center again, and then again as shown in the picture. Decorate your plane to celebrate African American achievements. Be creative!

Charles "Chief" Anderson, a famous black pilot, trained Tuskegee Airmen and once took Eleanor Roosevelt up for a ride!

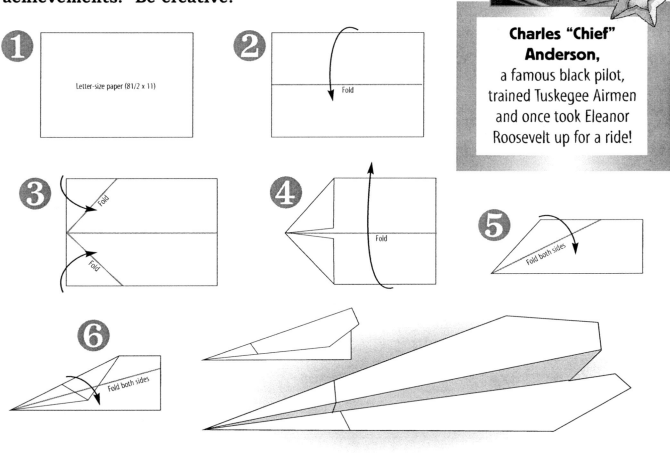

19

Japanese Internment Camps

In 1941, Japan bombed Pearl Harbor, Hawaii. For the United States, this was the beginning of World War II. Many Americans became suspicious of Japanese Americans because they thought they could be spies for Japan. Americans began moving Japanese Americans into camps. These camps were called internment or relocation camps.

Many years later, the government of the United States officially apologized for this action and paid reparations and claims to survivors.

Pretend that you were a Japanese American in an internment camp. Write about your feelings on your imprisonment and World War II.

A Japanese family from the Manzanar Internment camp

_____

_____

_____

_____

_____

_____

_____

Jackie Robinson

Jackie Robinson played a season of semi-professional football for the Honolulu Bears in 1941. After the Japanese attacked Pearl Harbor, he returned to the mainland and was drafted into the U.S. Army. After World War II, Robinson became the first African American player in Major League Baseball. From 1947–1956, Jackie Robinson played for the Brooklyn Dodgers. His civil rights activism helped create new opportunities for African Americans everywhere.

Little Rock Nine

In Topeka, Kansas, a black third-grader named Linda Brown had to walk one mile through a railroad switchyard to get to her black elementary school, even though a white elementary school was only seven blocks away. Her father tried to enroll her in the white elementary school, but the principal of the school refused. Other black parents joined Brown, and in 1954, the United States Supreme Court declared that students could no longer be segregated. The *Brown v. Board of Education* decision was a step toward integration.

From left, standing, are Ernest Green, Melba Pattillo, Jefferson Thomas, Carlotta Walls, and Terrance Roberts (next to Daisy Bates, president of the Arkansas Chapter of the NAACP). From left, seated, are Thelma Mothershed, Minnie Jean Brown, Elizabeth Eckford, and Gloria Ray.

Some public schools began to close rather than integrate. Many people started private schools in order to avoid integration. Still others defied court orders and remained segregated!

One of the most famous cases of integration was the Little Rock Nine, in Little Rock, Arkansas. The governor had the National Guard block nine black students from entering Central High in Little Rock because he didn't want to integrate Little Rock's schools. President Eisenhower heard of this and sent Federal Troops to protect the nine black students.

Write About It!

How does it feel to be the "only one"? Maybe you're the only boy or the only girl. Maybe you've been the only one with glasses, freckles, curly hair, or the only one who forgot to bring their permission slip to go on a field trip.

Write about a time when you were the "only one." How did it make you feel?

_____

_____

_____

_____

_____

Mother of the Civil Rights Movement

Today, Rosa Parks is sometimes called the "Mother of the Civil Rights Movement." She served as secretary of the NAACP and later Adviser to the NAACP Youth Council, and tried to register to vote on several occasions when it was still nearly impossible to do so.

In 1955, Rosa Parks took a very brave step toward integration and civil rights. After a long day at work, she took a seat on a Montgomery, Alabama bus, but she wouldn't give it up to a white man as the law of segregation required. Rosa Parks was arrested, leading to a year-long boycott of Montgomery buses. Dr. Martin Luther King, Jr. led the successful boycott which ended in 1956 with a ruling from the U.S. Supreme Court outlawing all segregated public transportation in the city!

Write the cause of each effect. The first one has been done for you.

1. Effect: Rosa Parks is called the "Mother of the Civil Rights Movement."

   Cause: Rosa Parks took a stand against segregation.

2. Effect: Rosa Parks was arrested.

   Cause: _____

3. Effect: The Supreme Court outlawed all segregated public transportation in the city.

   Cause: _____

4. Effect: Segregation made life difficult for Rosa Parks and many others.

   Cause: _____

   _____

WORD DEFINITION

boycott: to stop buying or using as a means of protest

Sit-in Protests

Ronald Martin, Robert Patterson, and Mark Martin are shown at the Greensboro "sit-in."

Sit-ins were important to the Civil Rights Movement. Up until then, African Americans had lived with segregation. They spoke against it, but no one did much about it. On February 2, 1960, four black freshman students at North Carolina Agricultural and Technical College (present-day North Carolina Agricultural and Technical State University) went into a Woolworth's lunch counter and they "sat-in." When told they would not be served because of the color of their skin, they refused to leave—this sparked a movement. The next day, they returned with 25 of their friends, sat at the counter, and were not served again. Black students in colleges throughout the nation saw it on television. They said "Why don't we go out and do the same thing?"

Answer the questions below.

1. How would you feel if you could not get service at a restaurant or a gas station?

   _____

2. How would you feel if the restrooms were closed to you but not everyone else?

   _____

3. How would you feel if you were thirsty, but were not allowed to use a drinking fountain?

   _____

4. How would you feel if you were required to use a different entrance to a building than everyone else?

   _____

5. What would you do if you knew someone else was being treated unfairly?

   _____

   _____

WORD DEFINITION

sit-in: to occupy a seat and refuse to leave a public place

23

Freedom Rides

Riders look on as their Freedom
Bus is engulfed in flames in
Anniston, Alabama

The Freedom Ride left Washington D.C. on May 4, 1961. It was scheduled to arrive in New Orleans on May 17, the seventh anniversary of the *Brown v. Board of Education* decision. The Freedom Riders wanted to test a decision made by the U.S. Supreme Court. The court had made it illegal for interstate travel to be segregated.

On May 14, the Freedom Riders split up into two groups. The first group was met by a mob of about 200 angry people in Anniston, Alabama. The mob stoned the bus and slashed the tires. The bus managed to get away, but when it stopped about six miles out of town to change the tires, it was firebombed. The other group was greeted by a mob in Birmingham, and the Riders were severely beaten.

Most of the Freedom Riders didn't make it to New Orleans. The few that did arrived by plane. Many spent their summer in jail. But they forced President Kennedy to take a stand on civil rights. The Freedom Riders gained respect for their bravery in great danger. The Freedom Rides inspired many others of the Civil Rights Movement!

Study the map. Write in all of the states that had Freedom Ride routes or stops.

Trace the route from Washington, D.C. to Birmingham, Alabama with a red pen or marker.

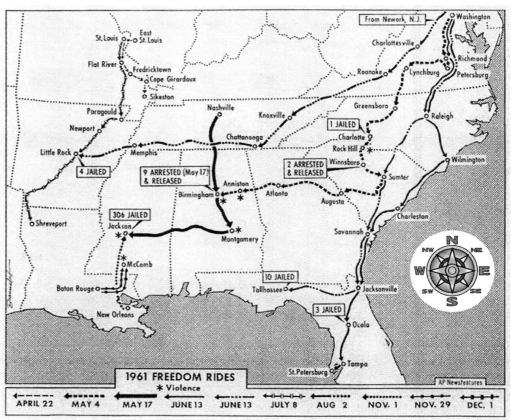

March on Washington

Blacks and whites, side by side, called on President Kennedy and Congress to provide equal access to public facilities and quality education for African Americans. Reverend Dr. Martin Luther King, Jr. delivered a famous speech in Washington D.C. Dr. King dreamed of a world in which black boys and girls could play with white boys and girls peacefully. This speech was presented on the steps of the Lincoln Memorial during the March on Washington. The march was a movement where thousands of people gathered at the nation's capital to protest inequality and racism.

Participants of the March on Washington crowd onto the lawn at the Lincoln Memorial while others relax and read the latest news. The headline reads, **"They're Pouring In From All Over."**

The success of the March on Washington was due in part to an effort to protest peacefully. Dr. King encouraged people to help protest unfair laws through peaceful means without violence.

Follow the directions to make an Origami Peace Dove! Use the pictures to guide your steps. Keep the dove to remind yourself not to discriminate against people who are different than you. Or give the dove to someone else as a gift of peace!

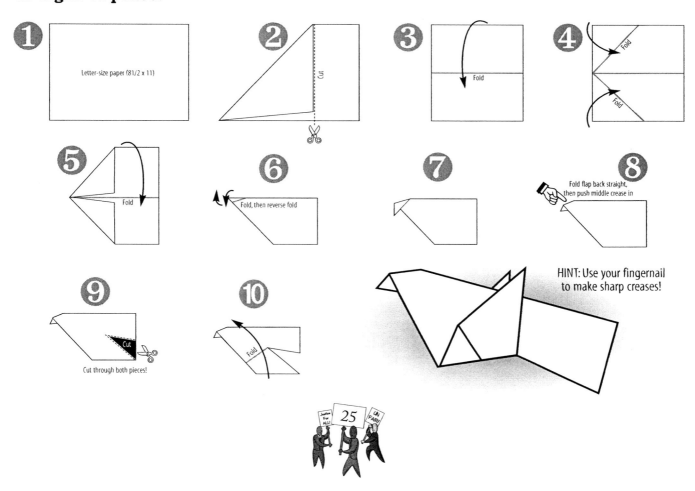

Civil Rights Leaders

Dr. Martin Luther King Jr.

One of the best known leaders of the Civil Rights Movement, Dr. King inspired many to join him in peaceful demonstrations. He received many honorary degrees as well as a number of awards, among them the Nobel Peace Prize. Sadly, Dr. King was shot on the balcony of a motel in Memphis, Tennessee on April 4, 1968. He was in Memphis to help lead sanitation workers in a protest against poor working conditions. In 1991, the National Civil Rights Museum opened at the site.

Dr. Martin Luther King, Jr. and Malcolm X

Malcolm X

Malcolm X was a controversial figure in the Civil Rights Movement. His views on relationships between blacks and whites changed in the 1960s after a trip to Mecca. He believed there could be a brotherhood between blacks and whites. When he returned to America, he founded the Organization of Afro-American Unity. In 1965, Malcolm X was shot and killed while giving a speech in New York City.

Medgar Evers

Medgar Evers began organizing local affiliates of the NAACP in Mississippi. He traveled throughout the state recruiting members and organizing economic boycotts. In June 1963, Evers was shot and killed outside his home. A white segregationist, Byron De La Beckwith, was charged with the murder but was set free after two different trials in 1964. He was finally convicted after a third trial in 1994.

Unscramble the letters below to find the word that ends violence.

A E P C E

These three African American leaders were all known for their work in the Civil Rights Movement. Sadly, they were all murdered by those who disagreed with them. Dr. King was a strong believer in "peaceful protests." On a separate sheet of paper, write about how the Civil Rights Movement would have been different if these leaders had not been killed.

Civil Rights Act

The Civil Rights Movement helped the passage of the Civil Rights Act of 1964. The act prohibits discrimination based on color, race, or religion in places like restaurants, hotels, motels, and theaters. Besides dealing with the desegregation of public schools, the act also made it illegal to discriminate in employment and prohibited discrimination on the basis of sex.

In 1963, President Kennedy was shot and killed in Dallas, Texas. Many leaders of the Civil Rights Movement were worried about Lyndon Baines Johnson as the new president. Johnson was a Southerner from Texas. Civil Rights activists were worried he might not support the movement.

On November 27, 1963, while addressing Congress and the nation for the first time as president, Johnson called for passage of the civil rights bill out of respect for President Kennedy. "Let us continue," he stated, promising that "the ideas and the ideals which Kennedy so nobly represented must and will be translated into effective action."

Write an "F" next to each statement that is a fact. Write an "O" next to each statement that is an opinion.

____ 1. Lyndon Baines Johnson was president after Kennedy.

____ 2. Lyndon Baines Johnson was a great president.

____ 3. The Civil Rights Act helped many African Americans.

____ 4. Poll taxes were used to keep blacks and poor whites from voting.

____ 5. Poll taxes are wrong.

FAST FACT!

The 24th Amendment to the U.S. Constitution outlaws poll taxes for national elections. This amendment forbids making voters pay a poll tax before they can vote in a national election. Some states once used such taxes to keep blacks and poor whites from voting.

27

Affirmative Action

In 1964, President Johnson gave two executive orders. They required government contractors and schools that received federal money to develop Affirmative Action programs. Affirmative Action is any policy or program designed to end discrimination against minorities and women (especially in employment and education).

The idea was that certain groups (especially women and minority groups) would be given special treatment when being considered for jobs, college admission, and other social benefits. Because there were no or few women and minorities in positions of power, many people felt this was necessary in order to give all people certain opportunities.

In the 1970s, some argued that Affirmative Action created "reverse discrimination." Some people felt that it was unfair for minorities and women to be given special consideration for jobs and other opportunities.

Arguments over civil rights continue today. The Civil Rights Act of 1991 reaffirmed the federal government's commitment to Affirmative Action. However, in the late 1990s, California and other states banned the use of Affirmative Action in state and local programs. But in 2003, a Supreme Court decision reaffirmed Affirmative Action in a case regarding college admission. They said it was OK to give special treatment to minorities in some cases.

Civil Rights Movement Interview

Find an adult you can interview about the Civil Rights Movement, then ask these questions. Record his or her answers below.

1. Which event of the Civil Rights Movement do you remember most? Describe the event.

2. How has the Civil Rights Movement affected you and/or your family?

3. What did you do to help the Civil Rights Movement?

4. When will the Civil Rights Movement end?

When Will It End?

Is the Civil Rights Movement Still Going on? Most people remember the great strides the Civil Rights Movement took in the 1950s and the 1960s. But don't forget who wrote, "All men are created equal..." — Thomas Jefferson way back in 1776. He was inspired by still earlier philosophers who wanted to ensure that people had certain basic civil rights. The civil rights of individuals have been an issue with government since the American Revolution.

In 1863, Abraham Lincoln remembered Jefferson's words in his Gettysburg Address. Lincoln also wrote the Emancipation Proclamation and helped with the 13th, 14th, and 15th Amendments which were designed to free the slaves and give them equal rights. Sadly, Lincoln was killed. While Lincoln did free the slaves, it was another 100 years before the Civil Rights Act passed!

In 1963, Dr. Martin Luther King, Jr. delivered his famous "I Have a Dream" speech at the Lincoln Memorial in Washington D.C. In his speech, Dr. King made reference to Lincoln's Gettysburg Address as well as Thomas Jefferson's Declaration of Independence. Dr. King reminded America of the words of her forefathers, and that Jefferson's words did not apply to all citizens.

Thanks to the efforts of leaders like Dr. Martin Luther King, Jr., Rosa Parks, and others, many laws and attitudes toward civil rights have changed. However, don't forget about the Civil Rights Movement. The Civil Rights Movement is a reminder that Americans must protect the basic rights of every individual now and forever!

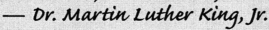

"I have a dream that my four little children will one day live in a nation where they will not be judged by the color of their skin but by the content of their character."
— *Dr. Martin Luther King, Jr.*

Additional Resources

America's Black Holocaust Museum

Located in Milwaukee, Wisconsin America's Black Holocaust Museum was founded by James Cameron in 1988 to educate the general public about the injustices suffered by people of African Heritage in America.

Manzanar National Historic Landmark

(better known as Manzanar War Relocation Center) was a Japanese American Internment camp during World War II that operated near Independence, California.

National Civil Rights Museum – www.civilrightsmuseum.org

National Historic Site – *Brown v. Board of Education* – www.nps.gov/brvb

NAACP – http://www.naacp.org/

BOOKS

Warriors Don't Cry by Melba Pattillo Beals (one of the Little Rock Nine). When Melba and a small group of other African American children attempt to enter an all white high school in Little Rock, Arkansas, they discover the harsh reality of prejudice and the true meaning of courage.

30

Glossary

abolitionist: one who works against slavery; someone who does not agree with slavery; a person who opposes slavery; a person who fought to end slavery

activist: person who fights for a cause; a very serious or militant advocate of a cause

amendment: a correction or change made to a document such as the U.S. Constitution; a change in, or addition to, a constitution, law, or bill

barred: kept out; refused entry

boycott: to join with others and refuse to buy, sell, or use something; refusing to buy a product to show disapproval of a company

civil rights: the rights of all citizens regardless of race, gender, or religion

constitution: the system of basic laws or rules of a government

emancipation: set free from slavery or strict control

martyr: person who suffers or dies rather than give up his beliefs

minorities: a small group of people of a different race or religion

movement: the actions of a group of people to bring about change

proclamation: an official public statement

social reform: change

veteran: a person who has served in the military, especially in a war; a person with lots of experience in an occupation or skill; a former member of the armed forces

Answer Key

Page 8: 1.F; 2.O; 3.F; 4.F; 5.O; 6.F

Page 9: Secret Word: Freedom

Page 10: 1. D; 2. B; 3. C; 4. E; 5. F; 6. H; 7. G; 8. A

Page 13: 1. Emancipation, freed, slaves; 2. Abraham, illegal; 3. soldiers, Union; 4. 40,000; 5. Civil, Southern; 6. 1863

Page 14: 1. 13th; 2. 15th; 3. 14th; 4. Answers will vary.

Page 15: 1. To become farmers, settlers, cowboys, and gunfighters; 2. Battle of Honey Springs; 3. unfair pay rate; 4. Buffalo Soldiers; 5. cattle thieves, bandits, and Mexican revolutionaries

Page 16: 1. a form of legal segregation; 2. Economic equality; 3. National Association for the Advancement of Colored People (NAACP); 4. European colonial powers

Page 17: 1. C; 2. E; 3. F; 4. D; 5. A; 6. B

Page 18: 2, 1, 3, 4, 5

Page 22: 1. Answer is given; 2. She wouldn't give up her seat; 3. Rosa Parks stood up for what was right; 4. People in power ignored the Civil Rights of the minority.

Page 26: Scrambled word: Peace

Page 27: 1. F; 2. O; 3. F; 4. F; 5. O

Index

abolitionists **10, 11**

Affirmative Action **28**

American Revolution **8**

Attucks, Crispus **8**

Buffalo Soldiers **15**

Civil Rights Act **5, 18, 27**

Du Bois, W.E.B. **16**

Emancipation Proclamation **13**

Evers Medgar **26**

Freedom Rides **24**

Garvey, Marcus **16**

Henson, Josiah **11**

Indian Citizenship Act **18**

Jim Crow laws **16**

King, Dr. Martin Luther, Jr. **22, 25, 26, 29**

Lincoln, Abraham **12**

Little Rock Nine **21**

Manzanar Internment Camp **20**

March on Washington **25**

Parks, Rosa **5, 22, 29**

Robinson, Jackie **20**

Sit-in protests **23**

Stowe, Harriet Beecher **10, 11**

Tubman, Harriet **9, 10**

Tuskegee Airmen **19**

Underground Railroad **9**

Washington, Booker T. **16**

Wheatley, Phillis **8**

women **17**

X, Malcolm **26**